Parenting

Is More Than

A FORMULA

JIM NEWHEISER

P U B L I S H I N G

P.O. BOX 817 • PHILLIPSBURG • NEW JERSEY 08865-0817

Scripture quotations are from the *NEW AMERICAN STAN-DARD BIBLE®*. ©Copyright The Lockman Foundation 1960, 1962, 1963, 1968, 1971, 1972, 1973, 1975, 1977. Used by permission.

ISBN: 978-1-59638-818-5 (pbk)
ISBN: 978-1-59638-819-2 (ePub)
ISBN: 978-1-59638-820-8 (Mobi)

Printed in the United States of America

I thank God for Pat, Christina, Don,
and Darlene for all the help they gave me
in preparing this booklet.

I am also grateful to God for all I have
learned about parenting from the writings
of my sisters in the Lord, Elyse Fitzpatrick
and Leslie Leyland Fields.

RECENT SURVEYS show that 60 to 80 percent of children raised in Christian homes drop out of church upon reaching young adulthood.[1] Parents are alarmed. They want to know what they can do to prevent their children from becoming prodigals. They yearn for a formula to guarantee that their kids will turn out right. Countless parenting books and seminars claim to offer the answer. The options can be overwhelming.

- As we begin, consider your own views on parenting. How should a family decide how to educate their children?

PARENTS ARE LOOKING FOR ANSWERS

Chip and Debbie reasoned that since they had gone to public schools and turned out all right, their kids should follow in their footsteps. They became concerned, however, when their eight-year-old son, George, started using bad words he had picked up in school. Then their ten-year-old daughter, Sally, began insisting that she be allowed to make the same entertainment choices as her peers. They were also concerned about the non-Christian perspectives taught in science and history. The last straw was when their children brought home a note from school telling them to come to class on Friday dressed in the colors of the rainbow for gay pride day.

Chip and Debbie decided to pull George and Sally out of the government school and put them in the local Christian school instead. They appreciated the commitment of the Christian teachers and administration and the effort to instruct the children from a biblical worldview. The tuition was so expensive that Debbie had to go back to work to pay the bills, but she was willing to make the sacrifice for her family. There were problems in the Christian school, however. Chip and Debbie were shocked to learn that the police had raided a wild party where several of the high schoolers were caught with drugs and alcohol. There were also rumors that the girlfriend of the principal's son had had an abortion during the summer.

Some friends then suggested that Chip and Debbie try homeschooling their children. Chip and Debbie liked the idea of having more control over what their children were taught and how they were disciplined. They also realized that it would be cheaper for Debbie to quit her job and teach the kids at home. Their own parents offered some resistance, warning them that they were going to ruin the kids. But they got lots of great advice, bought curricula, and set up a schoolroom in their home. At first George and Sally enjoyed getting to stay home, and they liked the less rigid schedule. But as they reached their teen years, George became resentful of his mother's bossing him around all the time, and Sally wanted to go back to the public school that most of their friends attended. Chip and Debbie started to wonder where they had gone wrong, and they had no idea what to do next.

- What might be some reasons that Chip and Debbie's approaches didn't work as they had hoped?

_____

_____

_____

- Did they do anything that you think was a mistake?

  _____

  _____

  _____

- Are any of Chip and Debbie's approaches things
  that you yourself have considered or tried before?

  _____

  _____

  _____

Mark and Annika both came from non-Christian homes. Mark's father was an angry man who would fly into a rage and beat Mark when he disobeyed. Mark determined that he would never beat his kids but would simply reason with them as intelligent human beings. By the time their son, Dirk, was four years old, Mark and Annika realized that this approach was not working. Whenever they tried to get Dirk to do something, he would throw a temper tantrum, often in public. Annika had a friend who gave her a book and some audios by an experienced Christian couple that taught a specific method for disciplining children. Annika and Mark listened to the audios and started to implement the system. Initially Dirk resisted the new regimen, but over time he became much more compliant. When their second son, Dan, came along, Mark and Annika tried to follow those same techniques, but for some reason Dan didn't respond as well. Annika's friend said she must not have been following the program well enough. Mark wondered whether they were still missing something.

- What might be some reasons that Mark and Annika's approaches didn't work as they had hoped?

_____

_____

_____

- Did they do anything that you think was a mistake?

_____

_____

_____

- Are any of Mark and Annika's approaches things that you yourself have considered or tried before?

_____

Bob and Diane had three children. Bob wanted to give his kids the best, both materially and spiritually. He made sure that his kids attended Sunday school every week and helped out with his church's midweek Awana program. He worked with his three children to make sure that they had their memory verses down letter perfect. In spite of all this Bible training, there was a lot of conflict in their home among the children and a lot of disrespect shown, especially toward Diane. Peter, a friend of Bob's from work, said that the Sunday school and Awana programs were the cause of the trouble at home because they pulled the family apart and undermined parental authority by having someone other than the father teach his children. Peter suggested that Bob and Diane come to his church, where the family was always together. There was no age-segregated Sunday school or youth program or even a nursery. This church equipped each father to be a patriarch and priest in his own home. Bob wondered whether this was the answer he had been seeking.

- What might be some reasons that Bob and Diane's approaches didn't work as they had hoped?

_____

_____

_____

- Did they do anything that you think was a mistake?

_____

_____

_____

- Are any of Bob and Diane's approaches things that you yourself have considered or tried before?

_____

_____

_____

Christian parents always want what is best for their children and are willing to make significant sacrifices in order to give them the best possible training. However, as we see in the examples above, it can be difficult for parents to pick which of the many available parenting formulas is best for their own family, and to predict what the results will be years down the road. They wonder, "Does the Bible teach a specific child-training methodology that guarantees that our children will grow up to be mature, productive Christian adults?"

MANY FORMULAS TO CHOOSE FROM

Many parents have relied upon educational formulas to ensure a good outcome with their children. In previous generations, parents trusted the public schools to give their children an education based upon Christian principles in a safe moral environment. Those disillusioned when court decisions forced prayer and religion out of the classroom have since turned to other approaches. Some have established Christian schools that incorporate prayer, Bible instruction, and a Christian perspective on learning. Many parents have made great personal and economic sacrifices to ensure that their children get a Christian education, with the expectation that these children will carry what they learn into adult life. Committed teachers have accepted lower salaries in order to serve the mission of the school. Other parents have become a part of the growing homeschool movement, devoting significant time and resources to preparing their children for adult life. Among Christian schools and homeschooling, various approaches such as classical education have been promoted as the key to preparing children to live as responsible, godly adults.

Parents have also put their hope in a variety of church-based formulas, believing that they are giving their children a solid foundation by taking them to Sunday school, children's programs, youth groups, Vacation Bible School, and youth camps. There is always the danger, however, of relying too much on the church while failing to provide training in the home, and the Family Integrated Church movement has tried to counteract this by teaching that any program that separates children from their parents is wrong and harmful. They say that the key to parenting success is for the father to teach his own children while keeping a very tight control on any outside influences.[2]

Parents have enthusiastically embraced different formulas for training and disciplining their children in the home. James Dobson's book *Dare to Discipline* made a huge impact when it came out in 1970.[3] Christians felt encouraged that a respected psychologist actually endorsed the spanking of children, as opposed to showing the permissiveness that characterized secular child-training theories of that time. Other experts advocate approaches to child training that claim to come straight from Scripture. Many babies and small children have been raised according to the Ezzos' *Babywise* and *Growing Kids God's Way* programs, which emphasize structure and schedule even from infancy.[4] Millions attended Bill Gothard's seminars[5] at which he authoritatively set forth steps for success when working with young people. Tedd Tripp's excellent book, *Shepherding a Child's Heart*, which has sold over a million copies, seeks to help parents go beyond controlling external behavior by addressing their children at a heart level.[6] Other parenting gurus, including Michael and Debi Pearl, offer detailed parenting advice to thousands of devoted followers.[7] More recently, books are being written that emphasize the role of the gospel and grace in parenting.

- What parenting approaches or formulas have you already considered? These could include educational approaches, church-based approaches, or home-discipline approaches.

_____

_____

_____

- What parenting methodologies did your own parents use?

_____

_____

_____

Strengths

Most of these formulas do have strengths. While it may not be as easy for Christian families to educate their children in a public school as it was when a good education with proper discipline and order was the public-school standard (as some of us are old enough to remember), some Christians still seek to be salt and light in these schools as teachers and involved families. Others are enthused about the new wave of public charter schools, which allow a high level of parental involvement at minimal expense. Christian schools can offer a high quality, biblically-based curriculum with faithful teachers who are committed to discipling their students. Still other parents have seen their children benefit from the individualized parental instruction offered through homeschooling and have helped them to excel academically.

Many unchurched young people have been led to faith through Christian programs for children and youth. These programs can also be helpful supplements to the training that children from Christian families receive at home. Children can be greatly blessed, especially as they come into their teen years, by adults in church programs who can speak scriptural wisdom into their lives (see Prov. 11:14). On the flip side, Family Integrated Churches rightly encourage fathers to function as spiritual leaders in their own homes.

Books and seminars about child training have helped many parents to establish discipline and structure in their homes. Those that have emphasized the need to address children at the heart level with the gospel, as opposed to merely controlling their behavior, have been a great help to many families.

- What are strengths of the parenting approaches you have used?

_____

_____

_____

- What are strengths of approaches you've seen *other* parents use?

_____

_____

_____

Weaknesses

However, most of the formulas also have their share of weaknesses. For instance, public schools often promote an antibiblical worldview in the classroom and provide a moral environment where temptation from ungodly peers is not uncommon. Even Christian schools can have an equally questionable peer influence.[8] Not all homeschool parents do an adequate job of educating their children. Others control their kids to such a degree that they are not prepared to take on adult responsibility.

Some parents are guilty of delegating the spiritual training of their children to the church and its programs. Some youth programs wrongfully separate young people from their parents and from the life of the church while also failing to provide sound biblical training. Children may memorize hundreds of Bible verses in order to win a prize, while their hearts remain untouched by scriptural truth. Yet those in the Family Integrated Church movement, who make their view of the family into a test of fellowship, have caused some good churches to split and have created new churches that can be like "gated communities" where those who don't follow their formula don't fit in.

A weakness of some child-training formulas is that they have focused on controlling behavior while neglecting the heart. Other formulas go beyond the Bible and fall into legalism.

- What are weaknesses of the parenting approaches you have used?

  _____

  _____

  _____

- What are weaknesses of approaches you've seen *other* parents use?

  _____

  _____

  _____

Various Results

On the one hand, proponents of each system can point to examples of success. There are many homeschooled families whose children are polite, accomplished, and bright. They go on to excel as godly young adults who are making a positive impact in the world. Christian schools often highlight their graduates who have gone on to academic and spiritual success. Many young people who attend public schools stand firm in their faith.

On the other hand, failures occur in each system. Some children in public schools get swept away into the world. Christian schools sometimes struggle with substance abuse and immorality among their students. Not all homeschooled kids have turned out as perfectly as their parents had hoped. One leader in the homeschool movement writes,

> I have heard from multitudes of troubled homeschool parents . . . that their children didn't turn out the way they thought they would. . . . Some of these young people grew up and left home in defiance of their parents. Others got married against their parents' wishes, and still others got involved with drugs, alcohol, and immorality. I have even heard of several exemplary young men who no longer even believe in God.[9]

- Why might the same educational or child-training approach have varying results for different children?

_____

_____

_____

- What was good and what was bad about how you were raised?

_____

_____

_____

- How did the way you were educated affect you?

_____

_____

_____

WHAT NOW?

Such varied results lead parents from formula to formula, looking for the silver bullet that will solve all their parenting problems. An experience of failure in one system often leads to the creation of the next.[10] Every year new books offer new formulas or fresh twists on old formulas. It turns out that the key is to teach children more about creation science or apologetics, claims one book. What really matters is that fathers spend time alone with each child every week, asserts another. Or we are told that we must teach our children critical thinking through studying the classics. One expert teaches that we can motivate children with rewards, while another warns that we will ruin our kids if we "bribe" them. Certain experts say that it is best to have big families, while others tell us that "the fewer children a family has, the more likely they are to produce spiritual champions."[11] One may be tempted to say, "Now that my children are grown, you tell me this?" or "I tried to follow the formula, but it didn't work with my kids." Leslie Fields writes, "You're parenting the best that you know how, guided by the best-selling Christian books, but your children are not responding. Why aren't they happy and content? What are you doing wrong? Why can't you create the peaceful Christian home so many promise?"[12]

- What has made you feel overwhelmed or hopeless in the approaches you've already tried or read about for your children?

With all the competing formulas out there, parents can feel overwhelmed when trying to choose the best way to train their children. There are four things to keep in mind that will help parents to choose what is best for their families.

I. EXERCISE DISCERNMENT

Parents need to exercise discernment when examining child-training formulas. Paul commended the Bereans because they examined the Scriptures to see whether what he and Silas taught them was true (see Acts 17:11). An expert's claim that his or her formula is God's methodology for child training is no guarantee. Parents who fail to be good Bereans may unwittingly buy into formulas that are either unbiblical or extrabiblical. Therefore, we need to distinguish between what seems plausible and what is actually proven from Scripture.

Anecdotal Stories Do Not Prove That a Formula Works.

Parenting books typically abound with accounts of families that have been transformed by following the author's methodology. They also give examples of the tragic results that occur when their advice is shirked. Such stories don't prove that these formulas are biblical or that they always work. In fact, there are always people who will say that they tried a given system and had bad results.

Scriptures Quoted by Experts May Not Prove What They Claim.

Even when parenting experts are able to "back up" their theories with handpicked Scripture quotes, discernment is still important for the Christian parent. I once heard a teacher use Matthew 1:18–25, in which the angel tells Joseph to take Mary as his wife, as a springboard for a message about betrothal. The speaker used this text as proof that families must practice betrothal (not even courtship), gave a detailed explanation of how betrothal worked in the first century, and reasoned that this provided a model for parents to follow when marrying off their children today. While some hearers might have been impressed because the speaker was using the Bible as the basis for his teaching, the Bible never actually teaches that we must practice betrothal. Furthermore, the speaker completely missed the purpose of the text in Matthew 1.

Another expert used the fact that Moses impressed upon Pharaoh the need for the entire nation, including their sons and daughters, to be allowed to go out to worship the Lord (see Ex. 10:8–10) as proof that churches should not have nurseries for infants or other programs for children and youth. This text has nothing to do with whether it is ever appropriate for the family to be involved in various programs in the local church.

Naturally, Christian parents want an approach that is based on Scripture, and when an expert seems to provide a biblical foundation, we may think we need to look no further. But, as with many positions, Scripture taken out of context can seem to support many parenting theories that it wasn't meant to support, and so a central Scripture quote isn't always enough to look for.

- Have you ever seen anecdotal evidence being used to support something that you still had reservations about or heard conflicting stories about later? What happened?

_____

_____

_____

- When have you heard people use Scripture to support dubious arguments?

_____

_____

_____

Parents Shouldn't Be Swept Along with the Herd.

Parents can be susceptible to peer pressure ("the fear of man," Prov. 29:25). When attending a seminar where the audience hangs on the speaker's every word, or when enthusiastic friends rave about a certain program, parents can feel social pressure to conform without critically analyzing the content that is being presented. Those who are insecure and who long for acceptance are especially vulnerable. They also can be tempted to be lazy, preferring to let an expert do all the thinking rather than taking responsibility to test his or her claims from the Scriptures.

Many Parenting Formulas are Legalistic.

The most dangerous kind of legalism is that which corrupts the gospel by claiming that our works contribute to our standing with God. Scripture declares that salvation comes by grace alone through faith alone in

Christ alone (see Gal. 1:8–9; 2:16; Eph. 2:8–9). There is another kind of legalism, however, that also harms God's people because it seeks to impose on them more than the infallible, all-sufficient Scripture (see 2 Tim. 3:16–17) commands. For example, I may tell a man that he should get a job and work hard to provide for himself and his family (see Eph. 4:28; 2 Thess. 3:12). But I cannot tell him that he must apply for a job at Walmart. The Bible encourages women to dress modestly (see 1 Tim. 2:9), but I can't tell a woman to wear a long, blue jumper with a white shirt and white tennis shoes when she goes shopping. "The important thing," writes Jay Adams, "is to always sharply distinguish God's commands from your suggestions."[13]

Parenting formulas become legalistic when they fail to distinguish between what Scripture explicitly commands on the one hand and what may be one of many possible ways to fulfill responsibilities to God on the other. "Some of the most popular books offer more than parental advice; they promise nothing less than instructions in raising children as God Himself would,"[14] writes Leslie Fields. They claim that their particular parenting methodology is God's way. Some have even gone so far as to say that God has revealed their parenting techniques to them, thus implicitly claiming extrabiblical revelation and denying the sufficiency of Scripture that equips us for every good work (see 2 Tim. 3:17).

For example, an author may write that a child's progress in potty training can be accelerated if the parent creates a chart on which a child can put stickers when success is achieved. Another expert may suggest that an effective spanking rod can be created by gluing together three wooden paint stirrers. Or an author may say that she found that putting her babies on a strict schedule and letting them cry in between feedings helped her children to sleep through the night at three months. Another may tell you to teach your children not to interrupt you when talking to adults, but to get your attention by standing next to you and gently touching your arm.

Each of these approaches may help some families, but the Bible does not say that we must use any of these particular techniques, nor does it promise that they will work for everyone. What the Bible teaches about parenting is quite simple[15] and is summarized in Ephesians 6:4: "Fathers, do not provoke your children to anger; but bring them up in the discipline and instruction of the Lord." Parents are then called to work out the implications of this in their own families.

When experts teach that their particular formula is "God's way" while failing to acknowledge that other approaches may be equally valid, they create extrabiblical "law." While we may all have our opinions, the Bible does not explicitly take a stance on the issue of putting a baby on a schedule rather than using demand feeding. Nor does the Bible promise that if you let your infant cry it out, he will be sleeping through the night at six months. The Bible says that parents should use the rod to discipline their children (see Prov. 22:15), but it doesn't specify the dimensions of the rod or the number or intensity of the swats for a particular infraction.

- What are some examples of legalism that you have noticed in different parenting systems?

  _____

  _____

  _____

- When have you felt "swept along with the herd," either with a parenting formula or anything else? What made you feel pressured?

  _____

_____

_____

• Write the parenting advice from Ephesians 6:4 in your own words. Why do you think this particular teaching is important enough to encapsulate the Bible's entire position on parenting?

_____

_____

_____

_____

_____

• What makes the kinds of legalism discussed above so dangerous and harmful?

_____

_____

_____

Extrabiblical Formulas Sometimes Fail.

You may have heard a parenting expert tell you to spank your child until he or she admits sin and is sweet,[16] but you may spend hours (or days) with a child who will not admit that he or she is wrong. Or, worse, the child may recite the expected apology without really meaning it. Parents may feel frustrated when they experience failure, questioning whether what the Bible teaches is really true. It can all seem so easy in a book or seminar in which many success stories are told. The problem, however, is not with the Bible but with the extrabiblical formula. There is no promise in the Bible that a rebellious child will confess his wrong and sweeten up quickly if you simply handle the situation the correct way.

Some Believers Impose Their Preferences on Others.

When believers or groups come up with their own extrabiblical rules and preferences and then try to enforce them on others, their efforts are often legalistic. There are churches that state in their bylaws that all members must homeschool their children. In other congregations, loyal members are expected to support the church's Christian school or youth programs. A family that doesn't share the dominant parenting philosophy of a church may feel unwelcome or even shunned. While the Bible teaches that parents are responsible for the training of their children, Scripture does not specify the exact methodology or the amount of outside help that a family should use. Whatever is not biblically mandated is a matter of parental choice for which parents are accountable before God.

In some contexts, the extrabiblical rules become elevated above what Scripture actually teaches and can create divisions among believers. Jesus warned such teachers that, "neglecting the commandment of God, you hold to the tradition of men" (Mark 7:8). Some parents won't let their children play with children who attend a public school. Other families won't let their children socialize with children who aren't being raised "God's way," that is, according to the principles taught by their favorite parenting expert.

- Think of some parenting tactics that sound promising to you. What are some elements of the tactic that aren't found in Scripture? How confident can you be that the tactic is certain to work?

  _____

  _____

  _____

- When have you felt excluded by the extrabiblical or legalistic rules that others have made?

  _____

- When have you seen believers become divided in these situations?

_____

_____

_____

Extrabiblical Formulas Fail to Take into Account Legitimate Differences between Children and Families.

Not every family is in a position to homeschool. Some don't have the financial resources or the skills. Others don't have the freedom. In many places, including China and Germany, homeschooling is illegal and parents may have their children taken from them if they try it. Stickers on a chart may not be effective in getting every child potty trained. Or they may work for a family's first three children but not the fourth. Some children may be more motivated by M&Ms. One author even suggests motivating a toddler to learn to use the toilet by taking him outside to hose him off when he has dirtied his diaper.[17]

Different children may be potty trainable (or able to sleep through the night) at different ages. You may meet parents who have trained five infants to eat and sleep on a schedule, but the same schedule does not work for the sixth.

When the man-made formulas fail, it does not mean that God and His infallible Word have failed. Popular Christian parenting methodologies represent human efforts to apply scriptural principles. There are usually alternate techniques that would be just as true to the Bible. While biblical principles are universally true in every era and cultural situation, man-made formulas often reflect the particular situation and experience of those who promote them. Parents must learn to distinguish between biblical principles and the various ways in which these principles might be applied. They must use discernment before fully committing themselves to any particular methodology.

• How can you be a good Berean when examining parenting methodologies?

_____

_____

_____

- What are some differences in personality or situation between your family and other families you know? Or between different families you've met? How might these natural differences make it difficult to apply the same parenting tactic to both families?

  _____

  _____

  _____

- Even if a parenting method is based as closely on a scriptural principle as it can be, why is it unwise to view it as *the* method that most correctly applies that principle?

  _____

  _____

  _____

- What is the key difference the author mentions between biblical principles and man-made formulas?

  _____

  _____

  _____

2. WHY DO KIDS TURN OUT THE WAY THAT THEY DO?

There was a believing couple who had two sons for whom they had high hopes. This couple sought to raise their sons to love and fear the Lord. As these young men reached adulthood, one son followed in the faith of his parents, but the other was stubborn and hot-tempered. The stubborn son committed a terrible crime, which resulted in his being separated from his family for the rest of his life. Of course, you know that the couple I speak of is the first couple, Adam and Eve. Why did one of their sons turn out to be godly, while the other became a rebel?

The Bible teaches that there are three primary factors that influence how children turn out.

Parental Duties

Parents are responsible to raise their children in the nurture and admonition of the Lord (see Eph. 6:4; Col. 3:21). First, parents are called by God to establish righteous standards in the home and then to discipline their children when these standards are violated (see Prov. 13:24; 22:15; 23:13–14; 29:15). Our children are by nature foolish. God has given us the rod to bring their foolishness under control. The rod is to be applied as a loving means of correction and is never to be used by an out-of-control parent in anger to exact revenge on a child (see Matt. 5:22; Rom. 12:19–21).[18] While we long for our children to be converted so that they will seek wisdom on their own, as long as they are in the home we are called to restrain their sin through consequences (see Prov. 26:3).[19] We are also called by God to train our children in His truth (see Deut. 6:4–25; Prov. 1:8; 4:1; 22:6). This training should be not merely moral, but redemptive, using their sin and ours to show them their need for the Savior. Parents also should be careful not to provoke their children to anger by sinful selfishness or inconsistency.[20]

Scripture teaches us that God blesses faithful parents and uses their influence for the good of their children (see Prov. 23:13–14; 29:17). The Bible also warns parents who are negligent in the training of their children that they are guilty before God of contributing to their children's ruin. "A child who gets his own way brings shame to his mother" (Prov. 29:15); "The father of a fool has no joy" (Prov. 17:21). The life of Eli the priest illustrates this concept. He was condemned for honoring his children above God because he did not stop them from doing evil (see 1 Sam. 2:12–17, 22–25, 29).[21]

King David also failed to restrain the evil of his sons Amnon, Absalom, and Adonijah (see 2 Sam. 13; 1 Kings 1:5–6), which led to dire consequences.

While parents do influence how their children turn out, they do not have absolute control of the outcomes. One may ask the question, doesn't the Bible promise that if you train up a child in the right way he will follow that way in adulthood (see Prov. 22:6)? The answer is that the Proverbs are not absolute promises, but rather are maxims that describe how wisdom generally works in the world. For example, Proverbs 10:4 says, "Poor is he who works with a negligent hand, but the hand of the diligent makes rich." This is a wise statement that is generally true; however, there are hardworking people who struggle financially because of droughts or disabilities, and there are sluggards who win the lottery. In the same way, godly parents often produce sons like Abel, but sometimes they find themselves raising Cain.

- What are the duties of parents, as commanded by the Bible?

_____

_____

_____

• What element should child-training have besides being moral? In your experience, do Christian parents focus more on this element, or on the moral element? Do you ever find it easy to forget this element yourself?

_____

_____

_____

• Since parents can influence their children but do not have absolute control over them, what does this tell you about the limits of *any* child-rearing formula?

_____

_____

_____

Each Child Is Responsible for the Choices He Makes.

Second, not all rebellion is the fault of parents. All children are born with a sinful nature (see Ps. 51:5; Prov. 22:15). Parents may seek to restrain their children's sin and point them to Christ. Yet it is the children themselves who must choose whether to embrace or reject the wisdom of God that their parents teach them. Young people will be subjected to other influences too, including the sinful inclinations of their own natures and the foolish temptations of the world. As children move toward adulthood, they are responsible for the fundamental life decisions that they make. The entire book of Proverbs is an appeal to the naive young person to choose wisdom over folly (see Prov. 1:18–33). A son who rejects his parents' training will encounter hardship and may die young (see Prov. 20:20; 30:11, 17). A child who heeds his parents' instruction will be blessed (see Eph. 6:2). A parent can faithfully instruct and warn his son, but he cannot make his son choose wisdom.

The case of Cain and Abel illustrates what happens in many families. Both sons were born with the same fallen nature and grew up in the same environment.[22] Each was responsible for the choice he made. Abel chose to worship God in a manner that pleased Him. Cain went his own way and even refused to listen to the Lord's rebuke (see Gen. 4:6–8). Ezekiel 18 illustrates how each generation is responsible for its own choice to submit to God or to rebel against

Him. A righteous father (see Ezek. 18:5–9) can have a son who rejects his father's ways and chooses evil (see vv. 10–13). But then the son of the wicked man may reject his father's sin and choose to be holy like his grandfather was (see vv. 14–18). In Deuteronomy 21:18–21, which deals with the treatment of an incorrigible son, it is not the parents who are blamed, but the wicked son who is executed for his wicked choices.

Just as the very first family was broken apart, Jesus warned that the gospel would divide families. "From now on five members in one household will be divided, three against two, and two against three. They will be divided, father against son, and son against father; mother against daughter, and daughter against mother" (Luke 12:52–53). Many Christian parents have shared the sorrows of Adam and Eve.

- Are we ultimately responsible for how our children turn out and for the choices they make? Who is?

_____

_____

_____

- What are some examples you have seen of children who have rejected their parents' lifestyle and chosen one of their own—for bad or for good?

_____

_____

_____

- What did Jesus mean when He warned that the gospel would divide families? What makes this happen?

_____

_____

_____

God's Sovereign Grace Is Needed to Save Our Kids.

Finally, and most importantly, both parents and children desperately need God's grace. There is no perfect parent! Even if our children were given to us as blank slates, we would make enough sinful mistakes to ruin them for life (see Heb. 12:10). Even if we were perfect parents, they are born sinners who could, like Cain, still choose to rebel (see Gen. 8:21).

There is no parenting book or formula that can guarantee that you can save your children. A child born in a Christian home is in as much need of regeneration as a child born in a Muslim family in Saudi Arabia. By nature they are dead in sin (see Eph. 2:1–3) and incapable of pleasing God (see Rom. 8:6–8). The Lord must draw them to Himself and give them spiritual life (see John 3:3; 6:37, 44; Eph. 2:4–9).[23]

At this point, parents may be wondering what they stand to gain by reading any further, if no parenting resource can give their children what they truly need! There is hope, however. God works in families and saves many children in Christian households.[24] He also saves children out of the most sinful, unbelieving homes. Later we will discuss how you can use common, everyday family situations as springboards to talk with your children about the gospel and to point the way toward the One who can truly save them. However, because our children's destiny is ultimately in God's hands, it is foolish to believe that through some parenting technique we can shape our children according to our own desires. Sadly, some parenting formulas falsely make just such a claim.

- Which of the three factors above is the most important of all?

- Why would it not make a difference if our children were given to us as blank slates? Or what could go wrong even if we were perfect parents?

- What does a child in a Christian home have in common with a child from an unbelieving home?

3. BEWARE OF PARENTAL DETERMINISM

Many parenting formulas imply that, if you follow their methodology, your children will turn out just as you dreamed, asserting things like "proper training always works with every child."[25] One "expert" writes, "Children are like bowls of warm, molten chocolate. . . .

Melted chocolate hardens into whatever shape it is dispensed into. If I tipped a bowl of melted chocolate onto the floor without a mold, I would have a wasteful, purposeless mess. If I pour the chocolate purposefully into a God-shaped mold I will have helped make something worth raving about."[26] Other parenting gurus declare that child training is as simple as training puppies or roses. One expert claims, "The training base we have described provides the certainty of a thriving garden of children."[27] The same expert admits elsewhere, however, "Not all homeschoolers become success stories. A few fail to measure up fully, while a small percentage fail miserably. Not all homeschool families create themselves equally. Homeschool children are the product of their parents and the culture they provide."[28]

Parental Determinism Is Not the Bible's View of Raising Children.

Actually, as we have already seen in Scripture, children are not merely "the product of their parents and the culture they provide." Children choose how to respond to their parents' training, and God must sovereignly work in their hearts to draw them to Himself. Leslie Fields warns, "We have adopted our culture's belief that we are the primary shapers of our children and that we have control over who they are and what they will become."[29] She quotes family psychologist John Rosemond, who declares, "Many of today's parents think they have failed if their children have problems. They think this because they believe in psychological determinism—specifically, that parenting produces the child. This is absurd. Parenting is an influence. It is not the be-all, end-all influence."[30]

- What is parental determinism? Give some examples and explain why it is wrong.

  _____

  _____

  _____

- What does the homeschooling expert imply about the children who admittedly _do_ fail at homeschooling, by saying, "Homeschool children are the product of their parents and the culture they provide"?

  _____

  _____

  _____

- What are some secular inspirations, mentioned in the quotes above, for the parental determinism view?

_____

_____

_____

Parental Determinism Further Damages Already Wounded Parents.

The implication of parental determinism is that successful parents will produce children who turn out well, while those whose children rebel are failures. One popular author claims that his research shows how parents can raise their children to be "spiritual champions."[31] Another asserts that "any parent with an emotional maturity level higher than the average thirteen-year-old can, with a proper vision and knowledge of the technique, have happy, obedient children."[32] What does this say about those who struggle with unhappy, disobedient children?

When parents who try a parenting formula experience failure, the experts defend the system by saying that bad outcomes are caused by parents' failure to follow the formula (that is, to keep the law).[33] You didn't shelter your children enough, they will say. Or you sheltered them too much. You didn't do nightly family devotions. Or you did them, but not in the right way. You homeschooled, but you didn't use the right curriculum. Or you had good standards, but you didn't set a good enough example or weren't consistent enough with discipline.

Hurtful (and unbiblical) statements are made about parents who "fail." For example, an otherwise helpful book includes this discouraging quotation: "I never saw a homosexual who had a good relationship with his father. We have come to the conclusion that a constructive, supportive, warmly related father *precludes* the possibility of a homosexual son."[34] The Bible, however, does not teach that being a good father necessarily determines that your son won't engage in a particular sin. I have counseled godly fathers, including pastors and missionaries, whose sons have struggled with homosexual temptation. I believe that if they were to read this quotation they would be unnecessarily devastated. There is nothing wrong with saying that a strong, godly father will have a good influence on his sons, but no father can control his son's heart and the choices that son makes as an adult.

If Parental Faithfulness Determines Outcomes, Is God a Failed Parent?

In the Old Testament, the Lord Himself is portrayed as the Father of rebellious Israel (see Ex. 4:22). He mourns, "Sons I have reared and brought up, but they have revolted against Me" (Isa. 1:2; see also Jer. 2:30; 5:3). Israel rebelled not because of the Lord's faulty parenting, but because of their evil choices. I find it comforting that God, the perfect parent, understands what parents of rebels are going through.

- What does parental determinism imply about the parents of both children who turn out well and children who rebel?

  _____

  _____

  _____

- How does parental determinism impose a weight of responsibility on parents that the Bible itself does not?

  _____

  _____

  _____

- What particular encouragement can parents of rebellious children take from God in His Word?

_____

_____

_____

Parents for Whom the Formulas Work Can Be Tempted to Pharisaical Pride.

Even though we know that God deals with us according to grace, we are all tempted to try to gain standing with God and men by our works. Parents can view their work as a means to achieve success and to gain respect from others. When our polite children all sit quietly in a row during church, each girl in her matching long dress and each young man with his bow tie and white shirt, we can see the admiring eyes. Some even whisper, "What a beautiful family." When other children rebel and get into trouble, we are tempted to judge: too bad they didn't follow the formula as well as we did. Some parenting experts repeatedly use themselves as examples of the pinnacle of parenting perfection, always saying and doing exactly the right thing with their kids (and even with the children of others), resulting in great success. "Deb and I raised five children with none of them ever rebelling against our authority."[35] They also tell stories of others who didn't heed their advice and who now taste the bitter fruit of their failures.

If your children are respectful, obedient, and walking with the Lord, give Him the glory. His grace alone makes you (and them) different from those who struggle (see 1 Cor. 1:30–31; 4:7).

Parents for Whom the Formula Doesn't Work May Be Tempted to Anger.

Parental determinism essentially says, "I followed the rules; therefore, God owes me." Nellie and her husband, George, came to me in tears because their twenty-year-old daughter, Gina, was pregnant out of wedlock. "I tried to do everything right," Nellie cried. "I quit my job to raise my children. I homeschooled them with the best curriculum. I kept them from bad influences. We had family devotions every night. How could God do this to me?" Nellie was angry with God because she had been taught that if she followed a certain formula, then God owed her a good outcome with her kids. Instead, she was living out her worst nightmare. Parents whose children fail to help them meet their desire to feel successful and appreciated can also become sinfully angry and embittered toward their children.

Paul Tripp writes,

> We tend to approach parenting with expectations as if we had hard-and-fast guarantees. We think that if we do our part, our children will be model citizens. . . . We tend to approach parenting with a sense of ownership, that these are our children and their obedience is our right.
>
> These assumptions pave the way for our identity to get wrapped up in our children. We begin to need them to be what they should be so that we can feel a sense of achievement and success. We begin to look at our children as our trophies rather than God's creatures. We secretly want to display them on the mantels of our lives as visible testimonies to a job well done. When they fail to live up to our expectations, we find ourselves not grieving for them and fighting for them, but angry at them, fighting against them, and, in fact, grieving for ourselves and our loss. We are angry because they have taken something valuable away from us, something we have come to treasure, something that has come to rule our hearts: a reputation for success.[36]

- How have you been tempted to make parenting success an idol?

_____

_____

_____

- How can this temptation be overcome?

_____

_____

_____

- What unreasonable expectation can parental determinism leave us with?

_____

_____

_____

Parents Whose Children Are Rebellious Bear a Heavy Burden of Guilt.

Fathers realize that they don't measure up to what the books say about the perfect dad who takes his boys hunting and his daughters on regular "dates," leads daily family devotions, runs his own business out of the house that he and his sons built, and helps his wife by teaching half of the subjects in their home school. Struggling dads could be disheartened when they read, "Why did some parents succeed and others fail? . . . The common denominator between success and failure seems to be the spiritual depth and sincerity of the parents, especially the spiritual depth and sincerity of the father."[37]

Mothers are told that they are "singularly responsible for who their children become."[38] They feel self-conscious when their kids act up around women whose children are well behaved. They feel pressure to be the perfect wife and mother who not only bakes her own bread, but grows her own grain and makes all her family's clothes by hand. She must teach her children with excellence in every subject while setting a Christlike example. When she becomes angry when her kids act up,[39] or when her perfect dinner for her perfect family isn't ready at the perfect time (and is burned), she feels like a failure. One mom, struggling with her own sinful impatience, lamented to me, "I homeschooled my children to protect them from bad influences, but who is going to protect them from me?"

Parents are told, "You must be all that you want your children to be,"[40] and "Good children grow out of good soil."[41] When parents see how far short they fall, they are tempted to wallow in guilt and despair, saying, "I have ruined my kids!" The experts state that your job is to be Christlike, and if you are Christlike, then your kids will turn out great. The problem is that we all fall far short of Christlikeness. Even if there were a parenting law or formula that could save our kids, it wouldn't help us because we are all incapable of keeping the law perfectly. All of us have been guilty of inconsistency, disciplining in anger, modeling sinful attitudes, and caring about appearances (that our children make us look good and so on).

- How does parental determinism cause harm?

  _____

  _____

  _____

- How can parents overcome the burden of guilt for their failures with their children?

  _____

  _____

  _____

- Why wouldn't it matter even if there *were* a parenting law or formula that could save our kids?

_____

_____

_____

Moralistic Formulas Can Also Create Children Who Are Little Pharisees.

Children, like adults, are prone to self-righteousness. They want to feel good about themselves by achieving an attainable man-made moral standard. A child thinks of herself as a "good girl" if she gets up on time, brushes her teeth three times a day (and flosses), gets good grades on her schoolwork, helps around the house, and makes eye contact with adults in conversation. There are many obedient, well-mannered young people who are still lost and may rebel once they become young adults. The outside of the cup looks clean, but the inside (the heart) remains filthy (see Matt. 23:25–26; Mark 7:6, 18–23). "Unregenerate kids are told that they are pleasing to God because they have achieved some 'moral victory.' Good manners have been elevated to the level of Christian righteousness," writes Elyse Fitzpatrick.[42] The danger is that self-righteousness actually keeps our children from the gospel because self-righteous children don't think they need a Savior. Jesus said, "I did not come to call the righteous, but sinners" (Matt. 9:13). Lane and Tripp write, "One of the reasons teenagers are not excited by the gospel is that they do not think they need it. Many parents have successfully raised self-righteous little Pharisees. When they look at themselves, they do not see a sinner in desperate need, so they are not grateful for a Savior."[43]

Deterministic Parenting Methodologies Will Ultimately Fail.

Parents who were proud at one point of their apparently successful efforts may be driven to despair when their children turn to the world. Children who were outwardly obedient when they were young often rebel when they reach adulthood. "We won't get the results we want from the law," warns Fitzpatrick. "We'll get either shallow self-righteousness or blazing rebellion or both. . . . We'll get moralistic kids who are cold and hypocritical and who look down on others . . . or you'll get kids who are rebellious and self-indulgent and can't wait to get out of the house."[44]

- How do moralistic parenting formulas produce children who are like Pharisees?

  _____

  _____

  _____

- How can children who "succeed" under a parenting formula actually be in a worse place than children who "fail"?

  _____

  _____

  _____

- What are the two camps our children will fall into if we raise them according to the law?

  _____

  _____

  _____

4. PARENTING IS ABOUT GOSPEL GRACE, NOT EXTRABIBLICAL FORMULAS.

While we are responsible to strive faithfully to follow God's parenting instructions, we cannot save our kids and (thankfully) we cannot ruin our kids. We are totally dependent upon God's mercy to us and to our children. There is no task in life that will humble you before God more than being a parent.

The Law Alone Will Not Bring Parenting Success.

Man-made rules have the appearance of wisdom, but they will not produce holiness (see Col. 2:23). We cannot establish the quality of our parenting by how well we keep the rules or follow a formula. Because we are sinners, we will always fall short. In the same way, our kids will not be saved if either we or they merely keep the rules. Some parents are consumed with making their children "good" when what they really need is the gospel. Their failure and inability to keep God's law is designed to drive them to the cross to seek grace (see Gal. 3:24). "*Moralism*—the idea that we merit God's favor by being good—is the deadly enemy of Christian parenting," writes Farley. "Moralism trusts in its own goodness, virtue, and principled intentions to get a 'not guilty' verdict from God on the day of judgment. It is deceptive. A cloak of morality over an unregenerate heart can make it difficult to discern the child's true spiritual condition."[45] Elyse Fitzpatrick writes, "Even if Johnny never burped at the table, it doesn't mean that he has right standing before God."[46] Earlier she says, "Most of us are painfully aware that we're not perfect parents. We're also deeply grieved that we don't have perfect kids. But the remedy to our mutual imperfections isn't more law, even if it seems to produce tidy or polite children. Children . . . don't need to learn to be 'nice.' They need death and resurrection and a Savior."[47]

Parents and Children Desperately Need the Gospel.

Parents must confess that only God loves and disciplines perfectly. We are going to fall short and will continually need God's grace to cover our sins and failures. We also need to plead for God to have mercy upon our children, who are sinful and foolish by nature. Our children can be saved only by the work of God. They cannot be saved by our good works of parenting, nor can they be saved by becoming "good kids."

Parents who realize that they also are lawbreakers will not be as prone to harsh anger when their children sin or make them look bad in front of others. Their children's sin will not surprise them (see Prov. 22:15; Rom. 3:20–23). Instead, they will use sinful failures as opportunities to declare the gospel. We are all sinners who need a Savior. Christ died to forgive our many sins (see 2 Cor. 5:21; 1 Peter 3:18) and to set us free from the power of sin in our lives (see Rom. 6; 2 Cor. 5:17).

Imagine if, the next time your child erupts in anger toward her sibling, rather than scolding her in your own anger, you used this as an opportunity to say, "I know you feel very angry right now. We are all tempted to become angry when we don't get what we want. Sometimes Mommy sins by being angry too. We both know that Jesus teaches that our anger is sinful. How thankful we should be that Jesus went to the cross so that our sins, including anger, could be forgiven and so that we could become more like Him! Let's read Ephesians 4:31–32 together before you go seek your brother's forgiveness."

While it is our duty to strive to be Christlike, it is just as important that we confess how far short we fall, so that we can point ourselves and our kids to our mutual need for Christ. "We cannot be Jesus; we can only need Jesus," writes Fields. "I fail in my efforts to be Jesus to my children because I am *not* Jesus. . . . Nor am I any kind of savior. I am a sinner saved by grace. . . . We don't even do the work of Jesus in our children's lives. We do the work of parents, which is to point our children to Jesus."[48] Dennis Johnson and Elyse Fitzpatrick add, "Rather than telling them that they can and will obey, we must tell [them] . . . that they cannot obey. They need help. They need Jesus."[49]

- How does using rules to try to make our children "good" actually go against what God's law was designed to do?

_____

_____

_____

- How will it affect our parenting when we keep in mind that we too are lawbreakers? What will it lead us to do and not do?

_____

- What is just as important as striving to be Christlike in front of our children? Why can this be difficult to do? Yet what makes it so important?

_____

_____

_____

How Does This Work Itself Out Practically?

As was mentioned earlier, the Bible's teaching on parenting is quite straightforward. "Fathers, do not provoke your children to anger; but bring them up in the discipline and instruction of the Lord" (Eph. 6:4). One Christian leader recently summarized it this way, "My three step parenting plan: spend time with my kids, don't kill them, teach them about Jesus."[50] However, all parents know that this straightforward plan translates into hundreds of day-in and day-out decisions, as they try to apply the "discipline and instruction of the Lord" to the real-life situations they encounter.

Here are some practical suggestions and guidelines to keep in mind.

Parents must establish discipline in the home by making expectations clear and bringing consequences for misbehavior. While the gospel is foundational in parenting, it does not eliminate the need for chastisement. Just as civil law restrains sin in society, discipline restrains sin in the home. For example, people obey the traffic laws not because they love the government, but because they don't want to pay a large fine. In the same way, the fear of chastisement can motivate a child who is still foolish and may not yet be a believer. The rod may also motivate a believing child to growth in wisdom. Fitzpatrick affirms, "Certainly children should be taught that pain is a consequence for disobedience."[51] When a five-year-old boy grabs a toy from his three-year-old sister and then hits her when she tries to get it back, he probably needs to be spanked. While the ideal might be that he would love his sister because he is motivated by Jesus' love for him, his behavior demonstrates that he hasn't fully embraced this wonderful concept. God has ordained pain as a means of helping him to abandon foolish and harmful behavior (see Prov. 26:3).

And yet, rather than merely spanking the wayward child, the wise parent will also use a child's disobedience as an opportunity to proclaim the gospel to the child. We shouldn't act shocked that our son has sinned. We, too, sinned as children and still struggle with sin. Sin should always remind both us and our children of our need for the gospel. We seek to avoid provoking our children to anger by humbly admitting that we, too, are sinners who continually need the gospel, and by seeking their forgiveness when we sin against them. Because we are unable to perfectly keep God's law, we need the work of Christ for forgiveness and to set us free from slavery to sin. "The Law has become our tutor to lead us to Christ, that we may be justified by faith" (Gal. 3:24). Elyse Fitzpatrick writes, "Every faithful parent *must* give their children guidance, directions, rules, and commands. What we are saying is that these things are not to be the primary theme of our teaching. The primary theme is to be Jesus Christ and the work he's already done."[52]

As we instruct our children in the Word of God, rather than just telling them stories and instructing them in moral principles (which they cannot follow in their own strength), we should seek to show them that God's plan of redemption is on every page of Scripture (see Luke 24:27). Several good books are available to help parents emphasize the gospel when teaching their children Bible stories.[53]

- How can parents incorporate the gospel into the discipline and instruction of their children?

  _____

  _____

  _____

- Why is discipline still a necessary tool for parents, even when they are being guided by gospel grace?

  _____

  _____

  _____

- Think of a specific disciplinary situation that you have encountered with your child, regularly encounter, or think you may encounter. How could you use this situation as an opportunity to illustrate the gospel instead of just imposing standards on the child?

_____

_____

_____

Gospel Parenting Is Not Merely a Formula.

Recently a mother brought her tearful seven-year-old son to me after the service. He was clutching a toy car in his little hand. "Tell the pastor what you did," the mom said. The little boy blubbered out, "I stole the car from the church. I'm sorry." I hugged him and decided to apply what I have been writing about.

"Tommy, I forgive you for taking the car and I am really glad that you confessed your sin. All of us, including your mom and I, also sin. When I was a little boy, I was guilty of stealing and of many other sins. Our sin reminds us of our need for Jesus. We all fail to keep God's rules. We can never be good enough. Jesus died on the cross so that His people's sins can be forgiven. And when we believe in Him, He gives us His Spirit to help us have the power to fight sin. Aren't you thankful for what Jesus did for us?" Tommy said, "Yes." After we talked for a few more minutes, I again hugged Tommy and encouraged his mother by commending her for her efforts to train her son. I hoped that our conversation might be used by God to draw Tommy to personal faith.

Two days later my wife and I went out to dinner with Tommy's parents. I asked how Tommy had been doing since our talk. His mom blushed and said, "Well, he stole another toy car from a friend's house yesterday."

While it is vital that we make the gospel central in our parenting efforts, we should not expect that grace parenting will produce immediate transformation in the lives of our children. We parents are in it for the long haul. We are not parenting for success. Rather, we strive to be faithful in pointing our children to Christ. We then trust God to work in their hearts to draw them to Himself, and in our lives to teach us more of His mercy and grace.

One of the benefits of having children is that they daily drive you to your knees as you realize your own weaknesses, sins, and inability to control outcomes. My wife and I pray together for our children every night before we go to bed, and we encourage the couples we counsel to do the same. You might pray something like this: "Oh God, please have mercy upon us, that in spite of our sins and weaknesses we might be faithful parents and somehow reflect the character of Christ to our children. When we fail, humble us and give us grace to repent before you, before one another, and before our children. When our kids hurt and disappoint us, help us to love them graciously as you have loved us. As you have shown us mercy please have mercy on them for Christ's sake. Amen."

- What should *not* be our goal in parenting our children?

_____

_____

_____

- What is our role in teaching our children, and what is God's role?

_____

_____

_____

- What, paradoxically, is a positive thing our children can help us to realize when parenting becomes discouraging? What important step does this always remind us to take?

_____

_____

_____

CONCLUSION: GOD IS AT WORK IN OUR LIVES THROUGH OUR PARENTING

Not long ago I listened to a recording entitled "Parenting in Weakness" by Dave Harvey.[54] I was surprised by his text, which was not from one of the famous child-training passages in Proverbs, Ephesians, or Colossians, but from 2 Corinthians 12:9–10.

> And He has said to me, "My grace is sufficient for you, for power is perfected in weakness." Most gladly, therefore, I will rather boast about my weaknesses, that the power of Christ may dwell in me. Therefore I am well content with weaknesses, with insults, with distresses, with persecutions, with difficulties, for Christ's sake; for when I am weak, then I am strong.

Harvey says that we once looked upon our parenting as a means to display our strength, but that God uses our parenting to display our weakness so that we might utterly depend upon His strength. I realized how true this is in my case. When my wife and I were preparing for marriage, we eagerly anticipated having children. As we thought of the mistakes our parents had made raising us and saw the examples of our friends at church, we genuinely believed that we would surpass them all. Just as Paul's thorn in the flesh kept him from being proud, the Lord has humbled us over the past thirty-plus years through our parenting endeavors. We have been broken by our own sins and weaknesses, often realizing that we could not measure up to what we knew we should be as parents. We have been humbled by the fact that we do not have the power to change the hearts of our sons. We have been humbled by many challenging situations in which we were not sure what we should do.

God has blessed us with several unexpected benefits along our parenting journey. He has given us a compassion for others who suffer, especially for those who grieve over lost and wayward kids. None of us has to pretend to be the perfect parent. Instead, we can openly share our struggles with one another. God has also taught us about love and grace. By loving children who have broken my heart, I have learned something of how God has graciously and sacrificially loved me, though I am completely unworthy. "But God demonstrates His own love toward us, in that while we were yet sinners, Christ died for us" (Rom. 5:8). God has used the exposure of my weakness in parenting to drive me to seek my strength and my identity in Christ, whose grace is sufficient for me.

Parenting is not about following a formula to accomplish your agenda for your kids. Through your parenting experience, God is at work in your life and in the lives of your children in ways beyond your present comprehension. We are not promised a particular outcome, but we are called to honor Him by being faithful to His Word. We and our children will often fail, which will remind us that our hope is in God alone. Leslie Fields writes, "Putting God first frees us to love our children more."[55] There are no guaranteed outcomes. If we put our ultimate hope in ourselves or in our children, we will wilt.

Thus says the LORD,
"Cursed is the man who trusts in mankind

71

And makes flesh his strength,
And whose heart turns away from the LORD.
For he will be like a bush in the desert
And will not see when prosperity comes,
But will live in stony wastes in the wilderness,
A land of salt without inhabitant."
(Jer. 17:5–6)

As we place our trust in God, which includes entrusting our children to Him, we can endure and even flourish, even when our parenting dreams aren't coming true.

Blessed is the man who trusts in the LORD
And whose trust is the LORD.
For he will be like a tree planted by the water,
That extends its roots by a stream
And will not fear when the heat comes;
But its leaves will be green,
And it will not be anxious in a year of drought
Nor cease to yield fruit. (Jer. 17:7-8)

- How do God's plans and purposes for our parenting contrast with our own?

- What are some ways the author mentioned in which even the discouragements of parenting have brought him unexpected blessings?

_____

_____

_____

- In what other ways might discouraging times or "failures" with our children enrich us and help us to grow in Christ?

_____

_____

_____

NOTES

1. See Cathy Lynn Grossman, "Young Adults Aren't Sticking with Church," USA Today, August 6, 2007, http://usatoday30.usatoday.com/news/religion/2007 -08-06-church-dropouts_N.htm; and "Six Reasons Young Christians Leave Church," Barna Group, September 28, 2001, https://www.barna.org/barna-update /teens-nextgen/528-six-reasons-young-christians -leave-church#.UhOfCorn_IU.

2. See the website for The National Center for Family-Integrated Churches at http://www.ncfic.org.

3. Dr. James Dobson, *Dare to Discipline* (Carol Stream, IL: Tyndale, 1970).

4. See Gary Ezzo and Robert Bucknam, *On Becoming Babywise* (Sisters, OR: Multnomah, 1993); Gary Ezzo and Robert Bucknam, *On Becoming Babywise: Book Two* (Mount Pleasant, SC: Parent-Wise Solutions, 2012); and Gary Ezzo and Anne Marie Ezzo, *Growing Kids God's Way* (Louisiana, MO: Growing Families, 1998).

5. The seminars were first called "Institute in Basic Youth Conflicts" and then "Institute in Basic Life Principles" (see "IBLP History," Institute in Basic Life Principles, accessed August 28, 2014, http://www. http:// iblp.org/about-iblp/iblp-history). Gothard's organization also has a regimented homeschool curriculum called Advanced Training Institute International (see their website at http://ati.iblp.org/ati/).

6. Tedd Tripp, *Shepherding a Child's Heart* (Wapwallopen, PA: Shepherd Press, 1995).

7. See Michael Pearl and Debi Pearl, *To Train Up a Child* (Pleasantville, TN: No Greater Joy Ministries, 2002).

8. This can happen because some parents of troubled kids pull them out of the public school and enroll them in a Christian school as a last resort.

9. Reb Bradley, "Solving the Crisis in Homeschooling: Exposing the 7 Major Blindspots of Homeschoolers," Family Ministries, accessed July 29, 2014, http://www.familyministries.com/HS_Crisis.htm.

10. For example, the failure of public schools led to the creation of Christian schools. Difficulties with Christian schools led to the homeschooling movement. Recent examples of failure among kids who were homeschooled has led to the Family Integrated Church model.

11. George Barna, *Revolutionary Parenting: What the Research Shows Really Works* (Carol Stream, IL: Barna Books, 2007), 22.

12. Leslie Leyland Fields, *Parenting Is Your Highest Calling and 8 Other Myths that Trap Us in Worry and Guilt* (Colorado Springs: Waterbrook Press, 2008), 4.

13. Jay Adams, "Legalism," Institute for Nouthetic Studies, March 7, 2013, http://www.nouthetic.org/blog/?p=2471.

14. Fields, *Parenting is Your Highest Calling*, 102.

15. Elyse Fitzpatrick points out that "in light of the number of books that have been written about parenting, the following statement may seem somewhat shocking: there are only two passages in the New Testament that give direct commands concerning it" (Elyse Fitzpatrick, *Give Them Grace: Dazzling Your Kids with the Love of Jesus* [Wheaton, IL: Crossway, 2011], 83).

16. "The chastisement is not over until a child is humble and has taken responsibility for his actions. It is only complete when his will is submitted to his parents" (Reb Bradley, *Child Training Tips* [Fair Oaks, CA: Family Ministries Publishing, 2003], 73).

17. Pearl and Pearl, *To Train Up a Child*, 71.

18. There is no better book, apart from Scripture, about the basics of child training than *Shepherding a Child's Heart*, by Tedd Tripp.

19. Much of our parental training operates in the realm of common grace. The law and its consequences restrain evil in those whose hearts are not yet renewed.

20. Lou Priolo's excellent book, *The Heart of Anger* (Amityville, NY: Calvary Press, 1997), addresses twenty-five ways in which parents can be guilty of provoking their children to anger (see chap. 2).

21. Eli did give his sons verbal warnings (as many parents today nag and whine at their wayward children).

22. We might add that neither had the wicked social influences of our day—evil neighbors, the Internet, MTV, and so on.

23. Christian parents should seek to faithfully proclaim God's Word to their children, which is the means by which the Spirit works in regeneration (see James 1:18; 1 Peter 1:23).

24. God's kindness in saving family members together is reflected in the households in Acts who believed and were baptized together (see Acts 16:31–34).

25. Pearl and Pearl, *To Train Up a Child*, 2.

26. Rochelle Melville, "Family Revolution," Signs of the Times, June 2007, http://www.signsofthetimes.org.au/items/family-revolution.

27. Pearl and Pearl, *To Train Up a Child*, 83.

28. Michael Pearl, "Jumping Ship (Part 1)," No Greater Joy Ministries, April 15, 2005, http://nogreaterjoy.org/articles/jumping-ship-part-one/.

29. Fields, *Parenting is Your Highest Calling*, 174.

30. John Rosemond, "Some Hard Facts about Child Rearing," The Washington Times, June 16, 2997, http://www.washingtontimes.com/news/2007/jun/16/20070616-082906-4321r/, quoted in ibid., 174.

31. Barna, *Revolutionary Parenting*, 152.

32. Pearl and Pearl, *To Train Up a Child*, iii.

33. They are something like the faith healers who take credit for any alleged success, but blame all failure on the

lack of faith of the sick person. Their system is proved by success, and it is assumed that every failure is a failure to follow the system.

34. William P. Farley, *Gospel-Powered Parenting* (Phillipsburg, NJ: P&R, 2009), 207–8.

35. Ibid., 33.

36. Paul Tripp, *Age of Opportunity: A Biblical Guide to Parenting Teens* (Phillipsburg, NJ: P&R Publishing, 2001), 35.

37. Farley, *Gospel-Powered Parenting*, 15.

38. Fields, *Parenting is Your Highest Calling*, 133.

39. Often it is the parenting perfectionism that contributes to the anger. When everything in the home doesn't go according to her plan and her ideal, she erupts (see James 4:1–2).

40. Pearl, "Jumping Ship (Part 1)."

41. Michael Pearl, "Jumping Ship (Part 3)," No Greater Joy Ministries, August 15, 2005, http://nogreaterjoy.org/articles/jumping-ship-part-three/.

42. Elyse Fitzpatrick and Jessica Thompson, *Give Them Grace* (Wheaton, IL: Crossway, 2011), 20.

43. Timothy Lane and Paul Tripp, *How People Change* (Greensborough, NC: New Growth Press, 2006), 5.

44. Fitzpatrick and Thompson, *Give Them Grace*, 36.

45. Farley, *Gospel-Powered Parenting*, 42.

46. Fitzpatrick and Thompson, *Give Them Grace*, 31.

47. Ibid., 17.

48. Fields, *Parenting is Your Highest Calling*, 134–36.

49. Dennis Johnson and Elyse Fitzpatrick, *Counsel from the Cross* (Wheaton, IL: Crossway, 2012), 164–65.

50. Kevin DeYoung, Facebook post, July 24, 2014, https://www.facebook.com/permalink.php?id=167207873110&story_fbid=10152290714223111.

51. Fitzpatrick and Thompson, *Give Them Grace*, 104.

52. Ibid., 29.

53. I especially appreciate the children's books written by Sally Lloyd Jones, such as *The Jesus Storybook Bible* (Grand Rapids: Zondervan, 2007) and *Thoughts to Make Your Heart Sing* (Grand Rapids: Zondervan, 2012); and Marty Machowski, such as *Long Story Short: Ten-Minute Devotions to Draw Your Family to God* (Greensboro, NC: New Growth Press, 2010) and *Old Story New* (Greensboro, NC: New Growth Press, 20120).

54. Dave Harvey, "Parenting in Weakness," The Institute for Biblical Counseling & Discipleship, June 23, 2011, http://www.ibcd.org/resources/messages/parenting-in-weakness/.

55. Fields, *Parenting is Your Highest Calling*, 59.

RECOMMENDED RESOURCES

Fields, Leslie Leyland. *Parenting is Your Highest Calling and 8 Other Myths that Trap Us in Worry and Guilt.* Colorado Springs, CO: Waterbrook Press, 2008.

Fitzpatrick, Elyse, and Jessica Thompson. *Give them Grace.* Wheaton, IL: Crossway, 2012.

Fitzpatrick, Elyse, and Jim Newheiser. *When Good Kids Make Bad Choices.* Eugene, OR: Harvest House, 2009.

Newheiser, Jim, and Elyse Fitzpatrick. *You Never Stop Being a Parent.* Phillipsburg, NJ: P&R, 2011.

Peace, Martha, and Stuart Scott. *The Faithful Parent.* Phillipsburg, NJ: P&R, 2011.

Priolo, Lou. *The Heart of Anger.* Amityville, NY: Calvary Press, 1998.

Tripp, Tedd. *Shepherding a Child's Heart.* Wapwallopen, PA: Shepherd Press, 1995.